**ANIMALS
IN
DANGER**

The Private Lives of Animals Series

ANIMALS
IN
DANGER

Translated by
IRENE R. ANDERSON

FREDERICK WARNE & CO LTD
London : New York

THE PRIVATE LIVES OF ANIMALS

HOUSE AND GARDEN
FIELD AND FARM
HEATH AND WOODLAND
POND AND RIVER
LAKE AND MARSH
MOUNTAIN AND VALLEY
TUNDRA AND ICE LANDS
SEASHORE AND COAST
SEAS AND LAGOONS
OCEANS AND DEEP SEAS
PREHISTORIC ANIMALS
ANIMALS IN DANGER

★

First published in Great Britain by
Frederick Warne & Co Ltd, London, 1976

© *Copyright 1974 by Casa Editrice AMZ e*
Produzioni Editoriali D'Ami, Milan, Italy

English translation
© *Copyright 1976 by Frederick Warne & Co Ltd, London*

★

Series Editor: RINALDO D. D'AMI
Text Editors: RINALDO D. D'AMI, LORENZO ORLANDI
Art Editors: CARLO ACCIARINO, FRANCESCO DAMASSO
Illustrated by: ANDREW W. ALLEN, ANGELO BIOLETTO, SERGIO BUDICIN,
    OLIMPIA BUONANNO, TINO CHITO, JAMES H. CRACKNELL,
    EDWARD S. DACKER, GIORGIO DE GASPARI, BRUNO FAGANELLO,
    EZIO GIGLIOLI, ANDRI LISIAK, BETTY MAXEY, ANTENORE SCHIAVON,
    GUISEPPE SIGNORELLO, GINO VIGOTTI, MARIA FAUSTA VAGLIERI,
    GUIDO ZUCCA
Research by: LORENZO ORLANDI
Designed by: PRODUZIONI EDITORIALI D'AMI

★

Text filmset in Great Britain by BAS Printers Limited
Printed in Italy by Stabilimento Grafico Marietti, Turin

ISBN 0 7232 1852 8

FOREWORD

When we look out of our windows and see sparrows and starlings, blackbirds and pigeons, and delight in the antics of grey squirrels that will sometimes take food from our hands, it is hard to believe that wild creatures are facing a serious crisis. But they are! Some 1000 different kinds of birds, mammals, amphibians, reptiles, and fish (not to mention nearly 20,000 wild plants) are estimated to be threatened with extinction.

A few of these species may be vanishing as part of the natural process of evolution (like the dinosaurs, millions of years ago, disappeared from the face of the earth because other animals evolved which were better adapted to life on earth and ousted them). But the vast majority of today's threatened species are in trouble because of man—and his activities.

Hunting (legal and illegal), the trade in both live animals and animal products, changing methods of agriculture, the demand for more 'living space' for man—and therefore less space for wild animals—all these are important factors. But all of them can be traced to the effects of an ever-increasing number of human beings on Planet Earth, and the growing demand by these people for a better standard of life.

Of course, it is 'only human' to feel that in any direct conflict of this kind, we humans must take precedence over animals. But the paradox here is that we humans are also animals . . . and we need wild animals, for our own survival. Some creatures, such as many bird species, help control insect pests which are problems for the farmer. Other animals, like the antelopes and gazelles of the East African grasslands, are much better adapted to life in some environments than the domestic cattle man has introduced, and could even be 'farmed' for man's benefit. We need wild animals because they give us pleasure. We need them because of their scientific importance. And we need them simply because they are beautiful—because without them our own lives would be so much the poorer.

The World Wildlife Fund is the leading international organization concerned with saving these vanishing wild creatures. We believe strongly that the future of mankind depends in a variety of ways on the continued survival of a healthy natural environment, and the wild animals and plants which share our world. The more that people everywhere know about these problems, the more chance we shall have of solving them, and so we welcome this book as an important source of information about what we consider the most important task of our time.

NIGEL SITWELL

Director of Information,
The World Wildlife Fund (British National Appeal)

CONTENTS

...four – three – two – one – zero!!

Every time that a rocket goes roaring up into space the animal life in the marshland surrounding Cape Canaveral in Florida seems to go mad. Great flocks of assorted herons, ducks and pelicans disperse in terror in all directions. Armadillos, alligators, snakes, otters and racoons hurriedly take refuge amongst the vegetation or in their holes. Then the fantastic space machine is swallowed up in the vastness of the heavens and the birds gradually settle once more on the grassy patches and on the pools and islets. And the other animals cautiously emerge from their hiding-places and resume their normal lives.

This is perhaps the most symbolic example of *coexistence* on the part of technological progress and nature; it is a compulsory form of coexistence reflecting the limits of what is possible here on Earth.

Present-day man needs technology, but he cannot do without nature. If the day ever came when there were no more birds in the sky, he would also have stopped launching rockets into space.

NATURE ADAPTING ITSELF

COEXISTENCE HAS LED TO DARK COLOURS

The peppered moth, *Biston betularia*, normally a light-coloured moth, blends in perfectly with lichens and the bark of the trees on which it is found, so escaping the notice of birds. Occasionally, darker specimens occur but are soon spotted by birds. In 19th-century England the smoke from the chimney-stacks in the early industrial areas killed the lichens and blackened the trunks, making the lighter moths noticeable. This gave the dark specimens an advantage in these areas. So there are now two varieties of this moth in existence. In industrial areas the sooty moth flourishes and in the country the light-coloured version.

As a result of pollution other species of moth are changing their colour too and so adapting themselves to environmental changes.

SOMETHING NEW

At one time the hedgehog, *Erinaceus europaeus*, was well known for its habit of picking up leaves and fruit on its pointed spines. Today this likeable little creature, attracted by the rubbish scattered about almost everywhere, may well be seen trailing a plastic bag along behind it.

PROTECTION OF KOALAS OR NATIVE BEARS

It is illegal to Kill, Injure or Molest any Koala or buy, sell or consign or have in one's possession or at one's disposal any Koala or the fur thereof.

—The Director of Fisheries and Hunting

This sternly worded notice has been put up on many trees on Phillip Island in the Australian state of Victoria, one of the repopulation areas created for koalas, *Phascolarctos cinereus*, when they were in danger of becoming extinct. The early Australian settlers made extensive use of the furs of these attractive marsupials and their numbers became reduced to only a few thousand, also as a result of epidemics and environmental problems.

Today it is calculated that there are more than 50,000 koalas scattered over the Australian continent. As you travel along by car you may happen to see them leaping from one tree branch to another along the roadside.

INTOLERABLE NOISE

Excessive noise, another scourge of present-day society, is responsible for insomnia and nervous disorders both among human beings and animals. Elephants working in the vicinity of an airport in Thailand became nervy as a result of the continual arrivals and departures of aircraft and have had to be fitted with special headphones that shut out noise.

The same device was used for a group of Asian elephants on their arrival at London Zoo, because the noise of low-flying jet aircraft was upsetting the poor beasts.

Living together: new ways of coping with modern evils

The problems of water pollution

CONTAMINATED WATERS
Effluent from urban centres and industrial areas pollutes rushing streams, rivers and lakes with fatal results, affecting fish life in particular. And the troubles do not end there, because most of this contaminated water ends up in the sea.

THE SEA

IMPENDING DEATH
The micro-organisms, jellyfish and certain types of fish living near the surface of the sea are those most exposed to the dangers of contamination, as solid particles of polluted matter become deposited in ever-increasing numbers on their respiratory organs.

OUT OF CONTROL
Exploration of undersea oilfields sometimes ends in large-scale ecological disasters. The gigantic bubbles of crude oil and natural gas, escaping from the control of the drilling teams, may pollute the sea for hundreds of square miles. Then the currents often carry these acrid, tarry slicks towards the coast, fouling beaches and rocks, and killing off fish, birds, marine mammals and other wild life.

Large-scale hunting for little treasures of the sea

IN DANGER OF DISAPPEARING

A marine top shell, *Trochus niloticus* from New Caledonia in the Pacific, has been intensively fished (more than 1000 tonnes gathered per annum) as a source of mother of pearl used for making pearl buttons. The survival of this brightly coloured ocean-dweller is now assured, thanks to the introduction of plastics and also to the strict steps taken to limit catches.

THE COLLECTING CRAZE

Owing to the beauty of their shells, many gastropods end up in the show-cases of collectors. To satisfy these enthusiasts, a flourishing trade is carried on, often to the detriment of various species of animals. The shells most in demand include cowries, of which we are showing a very fine specimen here, *Cypraea miliaris* of the Philippines.

THESE SCARLET FLOWERS ARE BECOMING VERY RARE

The red coral of the Mediterranean, *Corallium rubrum*, poetically referred to as the scarlet flower of the sea, has been used since ancient times as barter currency and for fashioning ornamental objects. Nowadays, this precious coelenterate has disappeared from vast stretches of the coast of Italy, France and Yugoslavia. This is due to the very intensive exploitation of coral, especially by sub-aqua divers who are provided with modern equipment enabling them to remain submerged for long periods.

Contaminators contaminated

SWORDFISH WITH A LICENCE TO KILL

In 1971, of 853 swordfish, *Xiphias gladius*, examined by the US health authorities in charge of food inspection, only 42 specimens were free from contamination by mercury, a substance with highly toxic effects on the human body. Tunnyfish examined thoroughly in 1972 also contained traces. The mercury apparently comes from industrial residues discharged into the sea. This is assimilated by the marine micro-organisms eaten by the small fish, which are then devoured by the larger ones. When eating contaminated fish, man therefore ingests the very poison that he himself has emptied so recklessly into the sea.

It hardly seems possible that the sea, that immense reservoir of life, should reveal signs of man's destructiveness.

And yet some marine ecological systems, especially that of the Mediterranean, have been seriously damaged by overfishing and pollution. The natural balance and the delicate relationships between the environment and its flora and fauna are upset thereby. The grave consequences of this also affect man who caused the damage in the first place.

The various species of marine animals are perpetually competing for existence. They are closely connected with one another like the links in a chain, so a decline in one species, caused, for example, by overfishing, may impair or promote the development of other species, throwing the "food chain" into disarray.

SOLAR ENERGY

The marine food chain is based on microscopic floating algae, *phytoplankton*. Utilizing solar energy and chemical substances present in the water, these unicellular organisms feed and multiply on a vast scale. So the source of food for *zooplankton* is being constantly renewed.

Some species of whales, the largest animals on Earth, feed on huge amounts of *zooplankton*.

THE LIFE-CYCLE OF THE SEA

Zooplankton, composed of tiny animals and the larvae of fish and crustaceans, is, in turn, a source of food for millions upon millions of fish, such as herring.

The remains of dead animals and vegetable matter fall to the bottom of the ocean and rot away. The chemical substances produced by the detritus rise to the surface where, with the help of solar energy, they are transformed into food for plankton, so renewing the marine life-cycle.

The herring serves as food for tunnyfish and marine predators.

The tunnyfish, in turn, may be devoured by voracious sharks.

The law of the jungle

THE FORESTS OF EUROPE ARE ONE OF NATURE'S BATTLEFIELDS

Herbivores are victims of carnivores: deer are caught, from the youngest age, by lynxes and wolves; rodents in general (but also birds of small and medium size and their broods) are consumed by lynxes, wild cats, martens, foxes, owls, hawks and badgers. The hedgehog, an insectivore, is devoured by foxes, wild boars, badgers and wolves but, if it is attacked by a viper, it is well able to defend itself and often kills that dangerous reptile, which feeds mainly on rodents. Ants and other insects which consume vegetable and inorganic matter are the normal food of birds. The bear and the wild boar, finally, are omnivorous and eat a mixed diet.

A revolving wheel

This shows in a simplified form how the life-cycle of the forest operates. Plants are eaten by herbivores and the latter by carnivores. The remains of vegetable matter and of herbivores and carnivores help to enrich the forest soil.

The diagram shows the close interrelationship between living organisms and also between them and their environment.

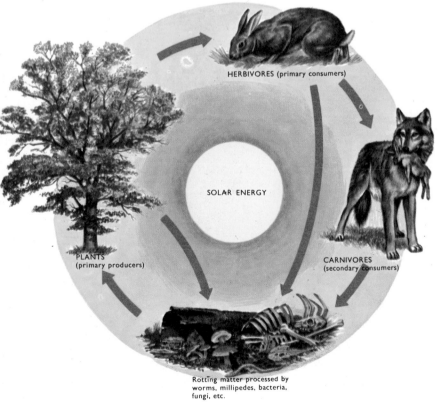

HERBIVORES (primary consumers)

SOLAR ENERGY

PLANTS (primary producers)

CARNIVORES (secondary consumers)

Rotting matter processed by worms, millipedes, bacteria, fungi, etc.

DIFFERENT ENVIRONMENTS, EACH WITH ITS OWN LIFE-CYCLE

The land as such provides a varied range of natural environments: woods and forests in the temperate zones, plains and steppes, deserts, marshes and pools, mountains, tropical forests, etc.

Each of these environments has a population of its own, in certain cases a large one, made up of different species. The result is a complete and comprehensive system governed by dynamic balances. If a single component is upset, that is enough to damage the whole system, sometimes with fatal results.

Every environment constitutes an independent ecological system, a self-sufficient kingdom in which the various species take on the role of food producers and consumers.

Great tit
(Parus major)

Red squirrel
(Sciurus vulgaris)

Peregrine falcon
(Falcus peregrinus)

Pine marten
(Martes martes)

Wolf
(Canis lupus)

Red deer
(Cervus elaphus)

European lynx
(Lynx lynx)

Nuthatch
(Sitta europaea)

Jay
(Garrulus glandarius)

Wild boar
(Sus scrofa)

Ant-hill of wood ants
(Formica rufa)

Green woodpecker
(Picus viridis)

Woodcock
(Scolopax rusticola)

Stag beetle
(Lucanus cervus)

Chaffinch
(Fringilla coelebs)

Bank vole
(Clethrionomys glareolus)

Common shrew
(Sorex araneus)

Viper
(Vipera berus)

European hedgehog
(Erinaceus europaeus)

Red fox
(Vulpes vulpes)

Results of upsetting the balance

If too many birds are hunted, there will be too many insects. If predators are destroyed, there will be more mice and vipers.

These are some examples of what can happen when man stupidly interferes and alters the natural balance. The incident shown below happened in Poland. The leading character in this drama is the otter, *Lutra lutra*.

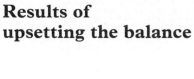

The otter catches the fish in a pool, eating the sickly specimens for the most part. The fisherman also catches large amounts of fish.

Fearing competition from the otter, the fisherman calls for the huntsman, who kills the otter.

Result: The sickly fish, no longer disposed of by the otter, spread an epidemic amongst the others and so the fisherman cannot find any more fish.

15

WE SHALL NEVER SEE THEM AGAIN

From time immemorial man has obtained a great proportion of his food from animals and it would be illogical to forbid him to kill the creatures necessary for his survival. But it must be borne in mind that scores of species have been exterminated for no valid reason. This wholesale slaughter was often motivated by greed for money and on other occasions by an unconscious urge to kill; or man feared competition from an animal species living in an area where new human settlements had been established. Pitting one's strength against lions, of which there were a great many throughout the Greek peninsula and the Balkans at the time of the Ancient Greeks, was regarded as a prerogative of noblemen, warriors and famous hunters. As Europe became populated and the forest areas dwindled, the lions declined in number until they finally disappeared altogether.

A REWARD OF £10,000

Widely distributed throughout the marshy savannahs of Thailand until the last century, Schomburgk's deer, *Cervus duvauceli schomburgki*, a magnificent animal with impressive antlers, was mercilessly hunted down even after the remnant that had survived took refuge in the jungle. There, in its last stronghold, it became completely extinct around 1930 and the reward of £10,000 offered by the British Museum for its skin and skeleton brought no result. Schomburgk's deer had vanished without leaving any trace.

SEEN FOR THE LAST TIME IN 1943

The last recorded sighting of the North African bubal, *Alcelaphus buselaphus buselaphus*, was in 1943, when some of them were observed in the savannah land of the southern Rio de Oro. The bubal was reared in a semi-domestic state by the Ancient Egyptians and they were still numerous in the south of Algeria until the beginning of the last century. They were pushed towards the Atlas Mountains as a result of colonization and disappeared between 1925 and 1930.

Now missing from Africa

A DEPRESSING RECORD

The first African antelope exterminated by the white man was the blaubok, *Hippotragus leucophaeus*; a bullet from the gun of a Boer hunter despatched the last of them in 1800. Those beautiful antelopes with grey-blue skins, of which there are now only a few stuffed museum specimens, were only found in the Swellendam region of South Africa in limited numbers, so the species was already in the process of becoming extinct.

EXTERMINATED

To cultivate the territories in which the quaggas, *Equus quagga quagga*, used to live, the Boer settlers wiped that remarkable subspecies of "semi-striped zebras" off the face of the Earth within a period of fifty years. In 1858 the last quagga from the region to the south of the Orange River in South Africa was killed. As for the herds living to the north of that river, they were slaughtered by new settlers who used their hides as sacks for storing grain. So the last quaggas disappeared between 1870 and 1880.

ANIMALS RESUSCITATED

CURIOSITY REWARDED
"I have always been curious," remarked the German professor of genetics Heinz Heck at the end of his well-known experiment. "Now I have achieved my desire."

A BRAND-NEW HORSE
Two species of wild horse, the tarpan of the woods, *Equus przewalskii silvaticus*, which became extinct during the 1700s, and the tarpan of the steppes, *Equus przewalskii gmelini*, wiped out in 1800, lived on the Eurasian continent. The first was the victim of deforestation and the second was ruthlessly hunted, also by breeders of domestic horses.

As soon as the experiment with the aurochs had been completed, the Heck brothers transferred their attention to the tarpan, or Przevalsky's horse. After selecting and crossing horses of various breeds, following the original characteristics, the Hecks produced a type of horse that was fairly similar to the one that used to gallop over the steppes.

THE ORIGINAL OX
Shortly before the Second World War the brothers Lutz and Heinz Heck, by crossing various breeds of cattle, tackled the problem of reproducing the aurochs, *Bos primigenius primigenius*, which became extinct in the 17th century. The result was a bull only roughly similar to the aurochs, a gigantic ruminant three metres long which appeared on this Earth 250,000 years ago. It is illustrated here with the elephant of the primeval forests, *Palaeoloxodon antiquus*. Hunted by prehistoric man and then by the Ancient Romans at the time of the wars against the Germani, the aurochs could be found throughout Europe and in North Africa and part of Asia. The last European specimen, a female, was killed off in Poland in 1627.

If man is to blame for the extinction of many animal species, it is also true to say that he must be credited with making attempts, partly successful, to "bring back from the dead" a couple that disappeared a long time ago. These are two wild mammals, the aurochs, a bull from which other domestic breeds were derived, and the tarpan, the wild horse of the Asian steppes, which can now be seen in the larger zoos.

CHICKS IN CHAINS

Years ago, owing to an unprecedented drought, followed by a disastrous flood, two million lesser flamingoes, *Phoeniconaias minor*, migrated during the mating season from Tanzania to Magadi, a Kenyan lake of volcanic origin, the waters of which are covered with a film of soda produced by evaporation. This did not worry the adult flamingoes, but incrustations formed on the legs of the young and, chained in this way, they seemed doomed to die. The prompt action of naturalists and of white and black volunteers saved over a hundred thousand of these small waterbirds.

HELPING NATURE

Action taken by governments and world associations for the protection of natural resources has already achieved good results. In many countries, parks and reserves have been set up, hunting has been controlled and certain animal species have been given complete protection to guarantee their conservation. Efforts to save the fauna and flora that are most at risk are becoming more and more concentrated and numerous, and cooperation between the various nations is gradually achieving greater efficiency. Appropriate centres are promoting programmes, gathering and checking information and distributing the aid needed to save what can still be saved, sending, not only the economic resources required, but technicians and scientists who can study the seriousness of the problem on the spot. Let us hope that man will indeed live up to his title of *Homo sapiens*.

RARE CHINESE DEER

Named after their discoverer, a French Jesuit who was able to admire them secretly in the imperial parks of the Forbidden City of Peking in 1865, Père David's deer, *Elaphurus davidianus*, became completely extinct in China in 1921. As good luck would have it, a large herd was built up from the sixteen specimens previously brought over to the park of Woburn Abbey. So other parks and zoos were gradually able to receive pairs of these very rare animals. In 1963 Père David's deer numbered over 400 in Europe. Some have even been sent to China, their country of origin.

From the Pole to the Equator, a competitive campaign aimed at prevention and cure

CHLOROFORMED CROCODILES

Hundreds of Nile crocodiles, *Crocodylus niloticus*, threatened by the increase in poaching, have been captured by African gamewardens by means of bait marked with coloured balloons. The large reptiles are dragged to the bank, anaesthetized and tied up, and subsequently wake up in a safer place.

SCIENTIFICALLY PROTECTED

In the last twenty years hunting for Polar bears, *Thalarctos maritimus*, became so well organized—expeditions were even arranged by European and US tourist agencies—that the number of these white plantigrades fell alarmingly. There were 10,000 specimens scattered all round the immense Polar Cap from Canada to Siberia.

To safeguard the species, of whose habits little is yet known, the Canadian Government has promoted research projects. A group of scientists, reaching an area inhabited by bears, put some of them to sleep by firing tranquilliser darts at them. The specimens caught in this way were carefully examined, weighed, numbered and then transported by helicopter to specially selected sites. Here their habits can be studied and this will make it possible for them to be more effectively protected in future.

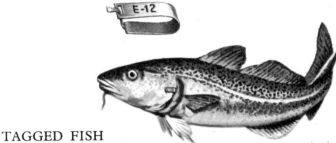

TAGGED FISH

Fish too, just like mammals and birds, have been marked. With these identity tags it is possible to ascertain, after they are caught, if the fish—in this case a cod, *Gadus morhua*—have remained in their distribution area or have migrated with other species.

RETURN TO THE VOLCANOES

One of the rarest and most extraordinary geese in the world is the Hawaiian goose, *Branta sandivicensis*, or nene. Unlike the other species, living for the most part in sub-arctic or temperate northern zones, this goose lives in the tropics. It does not migrate and prefers the rough lava beds of the Hawaiian volcanoes to an aquatic environment. Subjected for years to ruthless hunting, the poor nene reached the verge of extinction; in 1947 there were only about fifty left. Thanks to the painstaking efforts of the Hawaiian Board of Agriculture and the Wildfowl Trust, this fine bird is now officially protected and is thriving on the volcanic slopes of Mauna Loa, Mauna Kea and Hualalai, on the enchanting islands to which the species originally belonged.

Loving care

When—and this may be the fault of the commanding officer of an oil-tanker or the automatic self-steering equipment—hundreds of thousands of litres of petroleum pour out in a great slick over the sea and form a filthy and deadly coating along the shore, not even the birds manage to escape the suffering inflicted on marine life. The rescue operations carried out by the various associations for the protection of animals are in many cases highly effective and timely, even if the poor birds reach the shore in the same bedraggled state as the guillemot, *Uria aalge*, shown alongside. Some time ago, a whole colony consisting of thousands of jackass penguins, *Spheniscus demersus*, an attractive South African species, was contaminated by crude petroleum. The birds were attended to at once. After being sprinkled repeatedly with absorbent powder, over half of them were able to return to the sea after six weeks.

BIG-GAME HUNTING
IN THE DARK CONTINENT

Up to about the middle of the last century Africa was swarming with wild animals, just as if Noah had unloaded the contents of his famous ark on to the Dark Continent. But Europeans, who had started their slow advance some time before, moved steadily onwards, even entering the territories marked on the maps of the time with the words: "*Hic sunt leones.*" (Here are lions.) And so the explorers who opened up the way for colonizers did not merely come across lions, but a whole host of animals of every species. Just a few years later Africa came to mean a land where there was plenty of easy hunting to be had—with valuable skins, ivory and meat, all there for the taking. The colossal boom lasted for about a century, then this huge natural supermarket began to run short of supplies. With the end of colonialism the plundering and slaughter—this time the work of the native populations—increased. Perhaps stricter control and the establishment of new parks will enable us to save the African fauna, the living treasures of the Dark Continent.

THE RIFLE THAT NEVER MISSES
Apart from elephants, because of the very profitable ivory trade, the most savage big-game hunting has been directed against lions and the big cats with valuable furs, that is leopards and cheetahs. This has given rise to the romantic myth of the intrepid hunter of ferocious wild animals, of the white man with a rifle that never misses. Some have boasted that they have killed hundreds of animals.

ONLY WOMEN COULD SAVE THEM!
It is to be hoped that fur traders, who have been asked by various groups not to handle any more skins of tigers, leopards or cheetahs or any other animals in peril, will comply with this request. But how can we prevent smuggled skins from reaching the markets? The only solution would be for women to give up their very expensive fur garments. They alone could save the innocent and magnificent animals from extermination!

GETTING RARER AND RARER
Except in the deserts and the large equatorial forests, the cheetah, *Acinonyx jubatus*, once lived all over Africa and a considerable part of the Middle East, also in Turkestan and India. Today the Asian subspecies is almost extinct and in many African territories, where it used to be plentiful, the cheetah has become rare. Why? Because it is hunted for its

valuable spotted skin. The skins used traditionally by the various military bands will not be renewed. Here is a Kenyan Army drummer in his leopard skin. The model is showing a snow leopard fur coat. This Asian cat is one of the animals in peril.

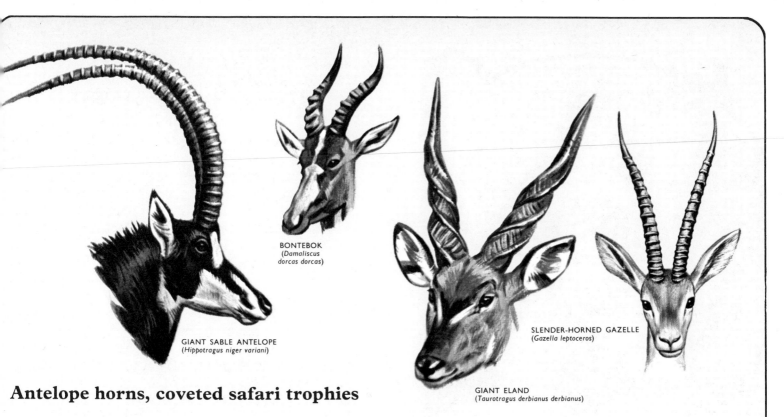

BONTEBOK
(*Damaliscus dorcas dorcas*)

GIANT SABLE ANTELOPE
(*Hippotragus niger variani*)

SLENDER-HORNED GAZELLE
(*Gazella leptoceros*)

GIANT ELAND
(*Taurotragus derbianus derbianus*)

Antelope horns, coveted safari trophies

A century of indiscriminate hunting has threatened the giant sable antelope, *Hippotragus niger variani*, of Angola, equipped with enormous scimitar-shaped horns, with extinction. There are little more than two thousand of them living under protection. The Swellendam Park in South Africa is the home of a thousand bontebok, *Damaliscus dorcas dorcas*, the last representatives of a species that was once abundant in Cape Colony. The giant eland, *Taurotragus derbianus*

derbianus, was for a time widely distributed in West Africa, from Senegal to the north of the Ivory Coast. It is a huge animal over three metres long and weighing a thousand kilograms, which, as a result of hunting and epidemics, is in danger of extinction. There are only about a hundred of them left. Finally, the slender-horned gazelle, *Gazella leptoceros*, a graceful inhabitant of the Sahara Desert, is becoming increasingly rare as a result of uncontrolled hunting.

An immense natural heritage is becoming exhausted

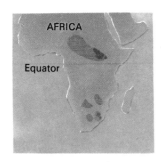

AFRICA

Equator

The area marked in red on the map shows the original distribution of the white rhinoceros. The areas in black represent the territories where it is still found today.

FOUR THOUSAND SURVIVORS
The French naturalist Buffon wrote away back in 1785 that "the rhinoceros fears neither the hunters' swords nor guns". If this statement were true, Africa would still contain a great number of these huge animals. But the largest species, the imposing white rhinoceros, *Ceratotherium simum*, is only now beginning to recover from the havoc inflicted by big-game hunting and slaughter by the natives. The two breeds of this species, one of which is spread through the Sudan, Uganda, the Congo and the Central African Republic and the other through South Africa and Rhodesia, now total more than 4000 protected animals.

POACHING, A DISASTER FOR AFRICA

Poison on the tips of spears and arrows, poison in the pools where the animals drink, traps of all kinds, nets, nooses, primitive and cruel snares, axes, firearms—these are the methods used by poachers, the last and most dangerous enemies of the African fauna. The record of massacres, started as soon as the nations of the Dark Continent gained their independence, is impressive: 20,000 leopards killed in the last five years, 12,000 elephants slaughtered in one year in the Tsavo National Park in Kenya, 100 animals of every species wiped out daily in a single reserve in Mozambique! This activity is so lucrative, especially the illegal trade in ivory, that organized poachers are able to bribe gamewardens and even some high-ranking officials. In certain areas of Kenya the coming and going of trucks, jeeps and government helicopters might well give the impression that the country is at war. But the government bans have not succeeded in stopping all this crazy and bloodthirsty killing.

"If this systematic campaign of destruction goes on," a head gamewarden said, "there will be no more elephants left in Kenya in five years' time." Let us hope that was not a prophecy.

SOUVENIRS FOR TOURISTS

On the arrival of the gamewardens the poachers have fled, leaving behind the macabre evidence of their raid on a Kenyan park—beheaded African buffaloes. The taxidermists would have stuffed the heads and sold them to tourists anxious to take an African souvenir back home with them.

A VICTIM OF FASHION

Gamewardens in motor launches patrol the Victoria Nile even during the night, because poachers hunting for crocodiles, *Crocodylus niloticus,* dazzle them with electric torches and finish them off by lunging at them with spears or shooting them. Unfortunately, the fashion world, which uses crocodile skins for the manufacture of a variety of expensive articles, has been responsible for an appreciable decline in the number of these reptiles in the rivers and lakes in which they were always so numerous. The inland waters of what used to be German East Africa, present-day Tanzania, were so thickly populated with crocodiles in the early 1900s that a reward of three rupees was paid for every one killed. In 1950 about 13,000 crocodiles were killed in Tanzania alone, but for some years now trading in their skins has been banned.

SMALL AND RARE

Deforestation in the strips of vegetation surrounding the large equatorial forests of Liberia has largely wiped out the striped duiker, *Cephalophus zebra*, a graceful member of the Bovidae just about forty centimetres high. There are no data on the number of these striped Artiodactyla still remaining, but in areas where they used to be common they are hardly seen at all now.

ALARMING SIGNS

Another "dwarf" in peril in the equatorial forests of Africa is the pygmy hippopotamus, *Choeropsis liberiensis*, a shy herbivore with nocturnal habits and having areas of distribution in Guinea, Sierra Leone, Liberia, the Ivory Coast and Nigeria. Unfortunately, the laws brought in to protect it do not seem to be safeguarding it effectively from hunting by natives and unscrupulous white men. Groups and pairs of these miniature hippopotamuses are becoming increasingly rare, an alarming sign that they are on the decline.

THE SCAPEGOATS

The Field Rangers are hard put to it to watch over the vast territories entrusted to their keeping. Poachers with expert knowledge of the area manage to find their way in without any trouble. The very high prices paid for the valuable skins and ivory (a native can live for a whole year off the proceeds from the sale of a pair of tusks) have caused an increase in poaching and raiding. The manpower used for African poaching consists of black men forced by their extreme poverty to break the law. If captured, they are the sole scapegoats for the rings of traffickers, who manage to send their rich consignments of skins and ivory out of the country in spite of all the bans.

25

GUINEA-PIGS FROM THE AFRICAN JUNGLE

Scientific research is helping to reduce the numbers of many animals, especially of certain apes and primates, because health authorities in various countries, medical committees attached to space-flight programmes and the large pharmaceutical industries require them for their experiments. So safaris organized for the capture of live animals are becoming more and more common.

A HAIRY HIGHLANDER IN DANGER

The existence of the peace-loving mountain gorillas, *Gorilla gorilla beringei*, which fluctuate in number between 5000 and 15,000 and inhabit a volcanic equatorial area between Zaire and Uganda, has been put at risk by the progressive destruction of the forests. Only by preserving the environment in which it lives can we guarantee the survival of this very shaggy primate.

AN ALARMING SITUATION

Destruction of the environment in the humid region to the south of the Rivers Congo and Kasai in Zaire is constituting a threat to the pygmy chimpanzee, *Pan paniscus*, the smallest and least known of the African primates.

TOO MUCH IN DEMAND

The long list of animals in peril includes the grey-necked rock fowl, *Picathartes oreas*, of the Cameroons, a rare bird from the equatorial forests whose existence is threatened by demands from zoos and private collectors.

AGRICULTURE IS TO BLAME

Owing to the extension of the areas under cultivation, the number of red Colobus monkeys, *Colobus badius kirkii*, which live only on the island of Zanzibar, has been reduced to just a few hundred.

BEHIND BARS

Zoos perform the worthwhile task of helping the public at large to get to know animals and in certain cases they have preserved species that would have become extinct if left in their free state. Unfortunately, the monotony of captivity, lack of space and loneliness slowly drive many of the animals mad, especially mammals. The leading zoos are, however, studying new ways of allowing their inmates to lead a more natural existence.

ANIMALS SOLD AS MERCHANDISE

At the present time the animal trade, that is the capture and sale of exotic fauna, is so highly organized that purchases can even be made by telephone. Firms specializing in this trade despatch their "goods" by air to and from all parts of the world and are also in a position to give advice about setting up zoos. Their best customers, after municipal zoos, are private zoos and circuses. But for every animal caught, from four to ten others are hurt or die. The actual journey, their inability to adapt themselves and the ignorance of the buyer result in further losses.

ITS FATE IS IN THE BALANCE

The mountain nyala, *Tragelaphus buxtoni*, spread over 150 square kilometres of the plateau of south-eastern Ethiopia, is a rare species of ungulate whose fate is in the balance. There are, in fact, hordes of poachers in the area and also bandits hunted by troops, all of them good shots and trigger-happy.

THE SUMATRAN TIGER

The reason for the disastrous plight of tigers belonging to the various subspecies that are scattered more or less all over the Asian continent are many — curtailment of their habitat, scarcity of their natural prey, hunting and poaching. In India, from 1939 up to the present day, tigers, *Panthera tigris tigris*, have declined from 30,000 to less than two thousand! A subspecies, that from Bali, *Panthera tigris balica*, can be regarded as extinct, although a few survivors may still remain there. As for the others, the Javan tiger, *Panthera tigris sondaica*, is represented by a remnant of ten or twelve, and of the Sumatran tiger, *Panthera tigris sumatrae*, smaller than the true tiger and with a magnificent coat bearing very close black stripes, only a few hundred remain in the forests of the large island of the Indonesian archipelago. Very high prices are paid by zoos for this extremely rare tiger.

THE MOST SOUGHT-AFTER CREATURES IN THE JUNGLES OF ASIA

THE EMBLEM OF THE PHILIPPINES

An impressive eagle is depicted on the national crest of the Philippine Islands, an appropriate symbol of that nation. It is the monkey-eating eagle, *Pithecophaga jefferyi*, so called because it feeds almost exclusively on those mammals. Today just about a hundred of these birds of prey remain scattered through the forests of the island of Mindanao. This is due to deforestation and hunting.

A WAR VICTIM

Little known by zoologists, the very lovely douc langur, *Pygathrix nemaeus*, must have been painfully aware of the chemical substances used to destroy foliage in the futile war of Vietnam, the very place where that monkey lives. We have no information about the present size of the population, but large sums are offered for its capture.

ALARM SIGNAL FOR THE ORANG-UTAN
The plight of the orang-utan, *Pongo pygmaeus*, is alarming. Only slightly more than 1000 live on the island of Sumatra and 4000 in Borneo; 600 more are housed in public and private zoos all over the world. The very high prices paid by zoos and science laboratories for the red primate have encouraged hunting, and the protective laws are having little effect.

IT MAY SURVIVE
Sparsely scattered over the Chinese mountains to the north and west of Hopei and in some regions of Shansi, the brown eared pheasant, *Crossoptilon mantchuricum*, has a very uncertain future in its country of origin. The survival of the species will perhaps be guaranteed by the birds being reared in European and North American zoos.

The craze for collecting small creatures

The collecting of small animals, a hobby that reflects a new and commendable interest in wild life and gives the owners a first-hand knowledge of nature, has an unfortunate draw-back. The demand for more and more exotic and unusual pets has grown, so increasing the likelihood of their becoming extinct.

A FROG AS A SOUVENIR
As a memento of a visit to the Valle de Anton, a natural hollow among the mountains of Panama, tourists took away thousands of tiny Panamanian golden frogs, *Atelopus varius zeteki*, which lived only in that area. The result is that this amphibian has almost disappeared.

WHOLESALE PLUNDERING
The rarity of bog turtles, *Clemmys muhlenbergi*, at one time distributed from Connecticut to North Carolina in the USA, is largely due to the demands made by collectors.

FEW GOLDEN SHOULDERS IN AUSTRALIA
Only 250 birds make up the entire population of golden-shouldered parrots, *Psephotus chrysopterygius*, or paradise parakeets, reduced almost to the point of extinction by dealers in cage birds.

AFRICA

VERREAUX'S SIFAKA
(*Propithecus verreauxi coquereli*)

GREATER DWARF LE
(*Cheirogaleus major*)

COQUEREL'S MOUSE LEMUR
(*Microcebus coquereli*)

RED-TAILED SPORTIVE LEMUR
(*Lepilemur ruficaudatus*)

A "LIVING FOSSIL"
Only fifty specimens make up the present population of aye-ayes, *Daubentonia madagascariensis*, the rarest of the lemurs. It has nocturnal habits and feeds on insect larvae which it extracts from the bark of trees with its very long toes.

MADAGASCAR:
THE DECLINE OF A UNIQUE MENAGERIE

The enormous slice of land now forming the island of Madagascar, which became separated from the African continent seventy million years ago, carried with it a nucleus of living things and in this way a unique collection of flora and fauna evolved through the years.

The depletion of this rare natural menagerie started well before the island became systematically exploited by white settlers. From ancient times, the native communities had ruthlessly hunted the extraordinary animals from the giant birds down to the small lemurs.

Now, with the intensive deforestation programme which has radically transformed a large part of Madagascar, the habitat of this primitive order of mammals has shrunk considerably. Fortunately, here too, as in other parts of the world, parks and reserves have been established *in extremis* to guarantee the survival of the species most at risk.

RUFFED LEMUR
(*Lemur variegatus*)

GREY GENTLE LEMUR or BOCOMBAL
(*Hapalemur griseus*)

DIADEM MONGOOSE LEMUR
(*Lemur mongoz mongoz*)

MONGOOSE LEMUR
(*Lemur mongoz mongoz*)

INDRIS
(*Indri indri*)

FORK-MARKED DWARF LEMUR
(*Phaner furcifer*)

BLACK LEMUR
(*Lemur macaco*)

AYE-AYE
(*Daubentonia madagascariensis*)

WOOLLY AVAHI
(*Avahi laniger*)

VERREAUX'S SIFAKA
(*Propithecus verreauxi*)

SPORTIVE LEMUR
(*Lepilemur mustelinus*)

GROWING RARER
The largest living species of Prosimii is the indris, *Indri indri*, which is ninety centimetres long. This lemur is fast becoming rare because of deforestation which is depriving it of its own special diet.

Once upon a time there was . . .

A BIRD—THE LARGEST THAT EVER LIVED

Until about the middle of the 1600s a giant called the great elephant bird, *Aepyornis maximus*, lived in Madagascar. It was about three metres tall and weighed nearly half a tonne and was too bulky to be able to fly. As this huge bird had no enemies on the island, except for crocodiles, its extinction was probably due to the gradual destruction of its natural environment, intensive hunting and plundering of its eggs.

Only a few years ago an elephant bird's egg laid 2000–5000 years ago was found intact. The egg of the aepyornis is the largest bird's egg known to exist, being over thirty centimetres long and nine kilograms in weight. It is equivalent to eight ostrich eggs and two hundred hen's eggs!

IT WILL NEVER CHIRP AGAIN

Sighted for the last time in 1843, Delalande's Madagascar coucal, *Coua delalandei*, a beautiful bird belonging to the Cuculidae which lived in the forests and on the ground, must be regarded as extinct.

THEY USE ITS TAIL

Insects, invertebrates, amphibians and small reptiles form the usual diet of this eupleres, *Eupleres goudoti*, a Malagasy mammal of the civet family with nocturnal habits. Scientists still know little about its behaviour. The eupleres is caught by the natives who use its thick tail as a personal adornment. It is also markedly on the decline.

Some have a hard time and others thrive on the large island

THE SCOURGE OF MADAGASCAR

Deforestation and the consequent extension of areas under cultivation have curtailed the numbers of many animal species on the large island, but others have benefited from these new conditions. One example is the Madagascar fody, *Foudia madagascariensis*, or weaver finch, which has found plenty of food among the local crops, especially in the rice-fields, and is multiplying at a tremendous rate. It has become a real menace. Flocks of fodies descend on the fields, lay them bare, strip the trees and even destroy the straw piled up beside the farm buildings.

This bird was introduced by man to numerous islands in the Indian Ocean and is causing the same damage there too.

CLEARLY ON THE DECLINE

A nocturnal predator that is very adept at climbing trees, where it preys on lemurs and birds, the fossa, *Cryptoprocta ferox*, about ninety centimetres long, is the largest carnivore in Madagascar. The fossa is hunted by the natives, who feed on its flesh, and it has been forced to move from the progressively dwindling forest areas, so that it is on the decline throughout the island.

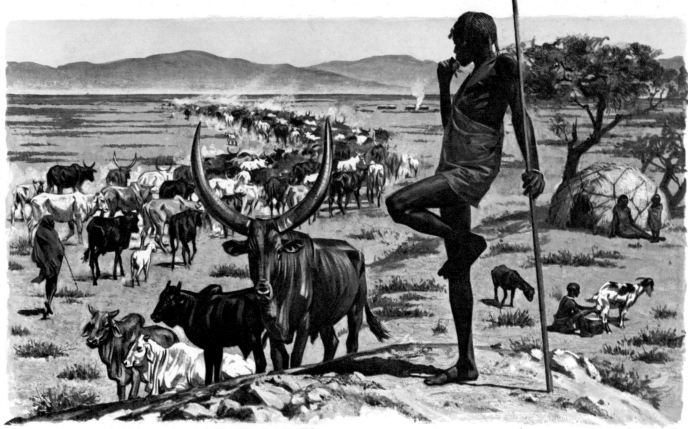

DOMESTICATED HERDS REPLACE WILD ONES

The large-scale rearing of domestic animals introduced by man to various parts of the world and their excessive use of grazing land has destroyed the natural environment for ever. For example, the very compact flocks and herds of sheep and cattle of the Masai in Kenya are constantly browsing and trampling down the area to which they are confined and are transforming the savannahs into an arid desert. Indeed, on the dust tracks trodden down by the herds vast cracks form after the tropical rains and the soil all around is becoming eroded. On the other hand, the wild ungulates that used to live in these regions and fed on all types of vegetation allowed it to grow again by shifting to other grazing grounds.

FAUNA INTRODUCED ARTIFICIALLY

For practical and sentimental reasons man has brought plants and animals from his place of origin to the countries where he settles, and continues to do so. This practice, carried on from ancient times, has sometimes been well tolerated by the new natural environment, but the indiscriminate introduction of newcomers has often led to serious imbalances, especially on islands, where the fragile ecological systems are more vulnerable than elsewhere.

It is calculated that about ten per cent of the animal and plant species existing today in a wild state were at some time introduced by man here and there in the world.

In recent years, thanks to the high standard of scientific research, it has been possible to transfer animal or vegetable species from one part of the world to another, to the great benefit of certain environments.

SAVING THE DATE-PALMS

Mauritania has brought out a stamp in honour of the ladybird, *Adalia bipunctata*, which has saved the date-palms infested with hordes of scale insects. The ladybirds were put into the plantations by French agricultural experts and devoured the harmful insects.

A SCAVENGER FROM CHINA

The grass carp, *Ctenopharyngodon idella*, belonging to the Cyprinidae family, was placed in certain rivers and canals to keep them clear of submerged vegetation. This fish is an avid feeder on water plants.

Dangerous immigrants

Man has not always altered the distribution of animals and plants intentionally; sometimes mice, insects and parasites of all species have travelled as stowaways on ships and even on aircraft and found themselves a suitable habitat at some port of call.

In many cases the indigenous animals have not been able to stand up to the vigorous and aggressive nature of the newcomers. The latter have prevailed and have eliminated their adversaries or reduced their numbers or forced them to change their mode of life in order to survive. Fauna transferred by man have, in turn, altered their habits and adopted a different pattern of behaviour to suit the environment. For example, animals that fed on fish and crustaceans in their country of origin have turned into predators attacking aquatic birds and domestic fowls.

TOO PROLIFIC
The starling, *Sturnus vulgaris*, was brought into North America, South Africa and Australia. It is very adaptable and extremely prolific. In fact, it has become so common that it is a menace to agriculture and to the other birds in those countries.

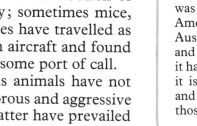

FROM AMERICA WITH GREED
The Colorado beetle, *Leptinotarsa decemlineata*, only slightly larger than a ladybird and just as pretty, reached Europe in the cargo of American ships in 1877 and has spread rapidly. Unfortunately, the damage done by this insect to crops of potatoes and other vegetables is tremendous.

INVASION OF FLORIDA
Some years ago millions of dollars' worth of damage was done to the vegetation in Florida owing to an invasion by *Achatina fulica*, a land snail 15–30 cm long that is prolific and also very greedy. The first three specimens reached America in the pockets of a small boy coming from Hawaii.

AN EXPERIMENT THAT FAILED
The Indian grey mongoose, *Herpestes edwardsi*, was introduced to Jamaica in 1872 to destroy the rodents devouring the sugar cane; however, it killed off, not only the rats, but also poultry, birds, reptiles, etc. The rats adapted themselves to living in trees to escape the mongooses which began to die out as time passed. So the plantations have been invaded by rats once again.

IT LIVES ONLY IN WONDERLAND

Large and heavy and unable to fly and with a stupid expression on its face, which was dominated by a huge hooked beak, the dodo, *Raphus cucullatus*, now exists only in the phantasy world of "Alice's Adventures in Wonderland". Harmless birds with little intelligence and incapable of defending themselves, the dodos were killed off by seamen who used them to replenish their shipboard supplies of fresh meat. Dogs, cats, pigs and monkeys brought on to the island of Mauritius by sailors and settlers also played their part by eating the eggs and young of these poor birds.

Of the twenty-eight species of birds that originally lived on the Mascarene Islands in the Indian Ocean, twenty-four at least were destroyed from the time when man landed in this paradise in 1600. This pointless extermination of living creatures, which is unequalled in any other part of the world, can be ascribed to the usual causes: indiscriminate hunting, the introduction of wild and domesticated animals belonging to Europe and Africa, and deforestation, carried out in frantic haste, also the capture of birds for commercial purposes.

ON THE ISLANDS OF THE INDIAN OCEAN

ANOTHER VICTIM

Hunted by the natives and settlers and by domestic animals brought into the island of Réunion, the Bourbon crested starling, *Fregilupus varius*, a lovely bird with a typical white crest on its head, disappeared around 1840.

THE LAST ONE DIED IN EUROPE

Caught in increasing numbers to satisfy the demands of bird fanciers in search of exotic species, the Mascarene parrot, *Mascarinus mascarinus*, disappeared altogether when the last specimen exported died in an aviary in Monaco in 1834.

FIFTY PAIRS
The entire population of black paradise flycatchers, *Terpsiphone corvina*, has been reduced to about fifty pairs living on the islet of La Digue (Seychelles).

DANGEROUS COMPETITION
In the last thirty years the population of Seychelles kestrels, *Falco araea*, has declined in an alarming manner and this small bird of prey, which at one time flourished, is today confined to the island of Mahé. The cause appears to be competition from a South African owl imported into the Seychelles to check the spread of local rodents which were having a very harmful effect on agriculture.

IT WILL PROBABLY BE SAVED
The black Seychelles Vasa parrot, *Coracopsis nigra barklyi*, is another of the birds in peril on the Seychelles. This rare species will escape extinction if the environment in which it lives remains intact.

THE GIANTS OF ALDABRA
Enormous, clumsy and defenceless creatures, the giant tortoises of the Seychelles, *Testudo gigantea*, caught in tens of thousands for over two centuries, are completely extinct in the archipelago. Today this species of reptile is still found on the island of Aldabra (Indian Ocean).

GARMENTS OF FEATHERS

The red iiwi, *Vestiaria coccinea*, a honey-creeper, caught in thousands because its feathers were used to make the multi-coloured ceremonial garments of the Hawaiian chiefs, has disappeared from many islands. Today the scarlet bird, which has been placed under protection, is plentiful only in the Hawaiian National Park and on the island of Kauai.

FROM THE PACIFIC TO THE ANTILLES ...

SURVIVOR OF SEVEN ERUPTIONS

Pritchard's megapode, *Megapodius pritchardi*, which incubates its eggs in the hot ashes of the volcanic island of Niua Fo'ou off Tonga, in the Pacific, and has survived seven eruptions since 1953, has a very precarious future because it is hunted by the natives.

IT IS PROTECTED NOW

Unable to fly and hunted by natives and Europeans for its feathers and also molested by dogs and pigs introduced to the island, the kagu, *Rhynochetos jubatus*, of New Caledonia was becoming increasingly rare; it has now been placed under protection.

THE LAST OF THE DRAGONS

The uncertain future of the massive and imposing Komodo dragon, *Varanus komodoensis*, or giant monitor, which is three metres long and is the largest representative of the Varanidae family, is governed mainly by increased feeding problems created by the natives' intensive hunting of deer and wild boars, the favourite prey of this reptile. The present number of dragons in existence on the three islands of Komodo, Rintja and Flores in Indonesia is estimated at around 700–1000, protected by appropriate laws. They will perhaps succeed in preserving this giant, which is terrifying in appearance, but as meek as a lamb.

AN UNFORTUNATE INSECTIVORE

Regarded as extinct in the last century, the Haitian solenodon, *Solenodon paradoxus*, an insectivore about the size of a rat, was rediscovered in the forests in the interior of the Dominican Republic in 1907. The increasing rarity of this small and unusual mammal with nocturnal habits has perhaps been caused, not so much by the mongooses introduced to the island a hundred years ago, as by developing indigenous communities who have progressively destroyed its habitat. Requests from zoos, prepared to pay high rewards for a pair of solenodons, have also contributed to the decline of this unfortunate species of insectivore.

... THE SAME SAD FATE

The trade in brightly coloured, talkative birds from the New World, which still flourishes today, was even carried on by pirates, many of whom kept them on board as pets.

HOUNDED BY ALL AND SUNDRY

Tracked down by dogs, seized by mongooses and even hunted by the natives for its flesh, the small Dominican hutia, *Plagiodontia hylaeum*, a herbivorous rodent about thirty centimetres long, survives only in the north-eastern portion of the Dominican Republic in very scanty numbers.

THE CUBAN FIVE HUNDRED

Relentlessly pursued by hunters, the Cuban crocodile, *Crocodylus rhombifer*, has disappeared almost entirely from the province of Matanzas and from the island of Pinos, where it used to be plentiful. The largest group, protected by very strict laws, is now concentrated in the swampy area of Zapata, extending over little more than one square kilometre; five hundred of these reptiles live there.

SEABIRDS ...

The varied and numerous species of seabirds inhabiting the rocky coasts, beaches, marshes and estuaries of rivers flowing into the sea have been hunted by man from the earliest times. In fact, these birds, which nest in crowded colonies numbering thousands of individuals, provided the primitive peoples with an easily available and plentiful source of food: meat and eggs. Hunting and also agriculture and industry in the last thirty years have led to the extinction of some species, while others are in grave danger.

STUFFED SPECIMENS IN MUSEUMS
The French explorer Jacques Cartier, landing on Funk Island off the north-east coast of Newfoundland in May, 1534, found such a large number of great auks, *Pinguinus impennis*, that "in less than half an hour"—as he wrote in his log-book—"we killed enough to fill two small boats". From then onwards these unfortunate birds, which were unable to fly, but were excellent swimmers and divers, were gradually slaughtered in ever increasing numbers throughout their distribution area, from the North Atlantic seaboard of America to the coasts of Scotland and Scandinavia. As well as eating it, seamen used the flesh of the great auk as fishing bait and even as fuel. In 1844, after three centuries, the species became extinct.

... IN PERIL

VERY RARE
There are now only about a thousand Audouin's gulls, *Larus audouinii*, living on the Mediterranean. The alarming decline in these birds appears to be due to the continual removal of their eggs by fishermen and by other species of gull.

THE SHOW IS OVER
An investigation has proved that in the course of ten years agricultural pesticides have caused brown pelicans, *Pelecanus occidentalis*, to disappear from the coasts of Texas and Louisiana. Their spectacular "nose-dives" into the sea to hunt for fish attracted thousands of tourists to the area.

HAS ANYONE SEEN IT?
In the last twenty years it has been sighted six times on the coasts of Texas and three times on the Atlantic coasts. The bird in question, the Eskimo curlew, *Numenius borealis*, was considered extinct after being killed for many years by hunters, but it is hoped that a small population has survived.

THE BERMUDAN SURVIVORS

Some years ago an ornithologist discovered on the island of Castle Roads in the Bermudas six nests of the Bermuda petrel, *Pterodroma cahow*, or cahow, a seabird about the size of a pigeon, considered to be extinct for 300 years as a result of ruthless hunting by the early settlers. Today the number of survivors has reached eighty and it is hoped that a larger cahow population will be built up in time.

THREATENED BY VOLCANOES

As a result of persistent hunting for eggs and feathers, the short-tailed albatross, *Diomedea albatrus*, is on the verge of extinction. More-over, on the Japanese island of Torishima, the only place where these large birds nest, there have been numerous volcanic eruptions which have fortunately claimed few victims among the hundred or so surviving albatrosses.

On tropical islands the white conquerors, in search of gold and silver, discovered

With the arrival of the white man in the tropical seas, their immense natural heritage began to dwindle and decline. The seas were teeming with animal life—fish and sea mammals; along the coasts there were plenty of crustaceans and the shores were dotted with turtles. Wherever those ancient mariners turned their astonished gaze they found a world of incredible plenty, an enchanted world which allowed itself to be touched and handled without putting up any resistance. The seabirds were so numerous and flew in such dense flocks that they darkened the skies. Once they had got over their surprise, the explorers began hunting and filled their ships with game, eggs and live animals. Then more came along—and still more. It was then the turn of the settlers, who spread over the most fertile and beautiful areas and sent for slaves to cultivate them. Today only a few remnants are left of what was once a luxuriant paradise.

innumerable bird colonies

THE STERILE EGGS OF BIKINI

The atomic explosions on the Bikini atoll in the Pacific had serious consequences. Affected by radiation, the eggs of the large colonies of seabirds that nest there, sooty terns, *Sterna fuscata*, and brown noddies, *Anous stolidus*, did not hatch, although the females sat on them. The birds went on laying until vast expanses of the atoll were literally carpeted with eggs from which no chick would ever emerge. Now, at last, the historic atoll has returned to normal.

SEABIRDS IN THE JUNGLE ▶

In the highest parts of Christmas Island, where the jungle is thickest and the trees reach a height of thirty metres, Abbott's boobies, *Sula abbotti*, can be seen on the topmost branches. This species lives only on this speck of land set in the Indian Ocean, and the entire population is made up of little more than four thousand birds, an adequate number to ensure continuity of the species if the island does not have to undergo the anticipated process of deforestation following upon the discovery of phosphates in the subsoil.

THE EXTRAORDINARY CREATURES ON THE GALAPAGOS ISLANDS

The Galapagos Archipelago, which came to the surface as the result of an oceanic upheaval occurring about a million and a half years ago, consists of fourteen volcanic islands presenting a desolate and monotonous appearance. The earth has little vegetation and is marked with craters and beds of old lava streams; luxuriant vegetation is only to be found on the high ground. In 1835 Darwin landed on the Galapagos Islands and their unique fauna—enormous tortoises, marine iguanas, birds incapable of flight and other strange creatures, including fourteen species of finch that were completely unknown—subsequently helped him to work out his fundamental theory of the origin of species. In little more than a hundred years, for various reasons, the numbers of some animals on these islands have declined considerably. But we trust that the Galapagos Islands, declared a national park by the Government of Ecuador in 1965, will manage to conserve their fauna, the only creatures in the world that are still trusting enough to let man approach them, just as in the days of Noah.

The Galapagos Archipelago, in the Pacific Ocean, is 800 kilometres from the coast of Ecuador, to which it belongs.

FERNANDINA
(Narborough)

ISABELA
(Albemarle)

THE THOUSAND THAT CANNOT FLY
In 1962 the population of flightless Galapagos cormorants, *Phalacrocorax harrisi*, was about 5000 and had by 1965 fallen to little more than 1000. This decline appears to have been caused by ruthless hunting and by theft of their eggs.

THREE HUNDRED DOCILE BIRDS OF PREY
No more than 300 Galapagos hawks, *Buteo galapagoensis*, docile birds of prey that calmly allow tourists near them, live on the Galapagos Islands. Newcomers to the islands, that is domestic cats, also pigs that have reverted to the wild, have contributed to their decline by competing with them for food.

CUTE MASCOTS
The capture of Galapagos penguins, *Spheniscus mendiculus*, by many yachtsmen and passing fishermen who keep them on board as mascots has reduced the number of these small and comical penguins on the Galapagos Islands to about a thousand.

the fascinating natural zoo that sharpened the awareness of a young scientist

PINTA
(Abingdon)

MARCHENA
(Bindloe)

GENOVESA
(Tower)

AN SALVADOR
(James)

RÁBIDA
(Jervis)

BALTRA
(South Seymour)

PINZON
(Duncan)

SANTA CRUZ
(Indefatigable)

SAN CRISTOBAL
(Chatham)

SANTA FE
(Barrington)

SANTA MARIA
(Charles)

ESPANOLA
(Hood)

A FEW HUNDRED GIANTS

Galápago, meaning "tortoise" in Spanish, was the name given by Iberian seamen to the islands of that archipelago, which, when it was discovered by them in 1535, was swarming with giant tortoises, *Testudo elephantopus*. Used first of all as a base by buccaneers and later by whalers, the Galapagos Islands became the main supply point for free provisions in the Pacific, as these huge and harmless tortoises, loaded in hundreds on to the vessels, guaranteed an ample stock of fresh meat for their crews.

But these reptiles gradually became less common. Now just a few hundred giant tortoises remain on the islands, but they are protected by law to ensure the survival of this species.

CATS ARE TO BLAME

A probable victim of domestic cats possibly brought to the Galapagos Islands by pirates, one of the local forms of Darwin's finch, *Geospiza difficilis debilirostris*, has become extinct on the Island of Santa Cruz and now survives only on San Salvador Island.

VALUABLE SKIN AND EDIBLE FLESH

Hunted down by seamen and settlers because of its valuable skin and edible flesh, and pursued by cats that had reverted to a wild state, the land iguana, *Conolophus subcristatus*, can be found on some islands, but has disappeared entirely from others.

45

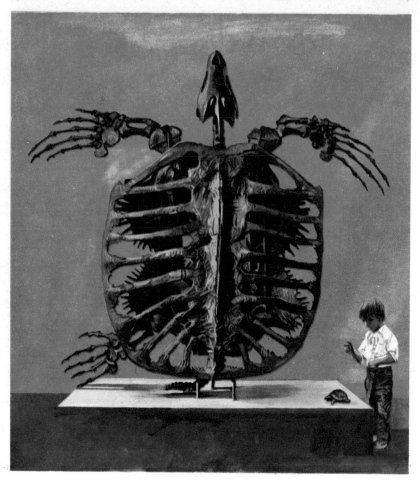

MARINE REPTILES

The life of marine reptiles, a group of creatures almost completely aquatic in their habits, is becoming more and more difficult and their future is full of uncertainties. Animals whose best chances of survival are in the sea are also tied to the land. To this they have to return to lay their eggs and relax in the sun after their extremely long and mysterious ocean voyages and, in the case of salt-water crocodiles, they also seek out suitable prey on land. Unfortunately, both turtles and crocodiles are being continually hunted down by man for their eggs, flesh, carapaces and skins. These destructive operations, which are proceeding on an increasingly large scale, can be stopped only by the strict enforcement of protective laws.

WILL THEY END UP LIKE THIS?
It is to be hoped that our present marine reptiles will survive and the continuity of their species can be guaranteed, and that they will not end up like this archelon skeleton from a giant turtle that lived in the seas of Kansas about seventy million years ago, and be put in a natural history museum.

A VORACIOUS SWIMMER
Extremely voracious and an excellent swimmer capable of covering hundreds of kilometres out in the open sea, the salt-water crocodile, *Crocodylus porosus*, is a monster actually seven and a half metres long. It has been slaughtered for its valuable skin, but nowadays, in Australia at least, it is protected and hunters need a special permit. Its distribution area covers two continents.

PROTECTED, BUT STILL HUNTED
For thousands of years turtles have persisted in their ancestral custom of always going to lay their eggs on the same sandy beaches. This readily exposes the reptiles to attack by local communities who rob them of their eggs or catch them and eat them. An example of this is the green turtle, *Chelonia mydas*, one of the species most at risk because of its very tasty flesh. It has virtually disappeared from the Antilles area, where it used to be abundant, and is showing a serious decline in other regions. Vigorous steps have been taken to safeguard the species in Central America and Indonesia, where its reproduction areas are watched, but this large turtle is still waylaid by the fishermen of the warm seas where it lives and it is attacked by sub-aqua hunters, who are becoming more and more numerous.

past, present and an uncertain future

Only by setting up suitable reserves, that is reproduction sites, for the leathery turtle, *Dermochelys coriacea*, a creature distributed nearly all over the world a century ago, will it be possible to save this over-exploited species.

The growing demand for its abdominal cartilage for the soap industry, its flesh for the preparation of tasty soup and its oil for the manufacture of cosmetics is seriously threatening the hawksbill turtle, *Eretmochelys imbricata*, with extinction.

The Mexican Government has extended its protection to the loggerhead turtle, *Lepidochelys kempi*, which was pursued so relentlessly that there were fears that it would not survive. ➤

SOS FOR THE OCEAN GIANTS

Until a century ago whales were still as numerous in seas all over the world as bison on the American prairies. Now, a hundred years after the start of the organized whaling industry, these leviathans of the deep have declined in number to such an extent that whalers are being forced to hunt for the smaller and less profitable species.

It is amazing that such gigantic mammals, which have no natural enemies and spend their whole time cruising mysteriously through polar and equatorial waters, should be condemned to extinction, as the bulk of the products obtained from them, except for their meat, have long since been superseded. But the organized carnage continues, because the nations concerned will not observe the restrictions imposed and it is quite impossible to keep a check on the large and small whalers processing the "raw material" out in the open sea.

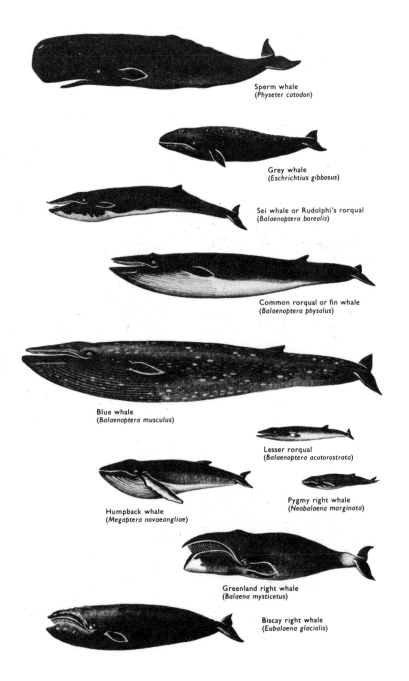

Sperm whale
(*Physeter catodon*)

Grey whale
(*Eschrichtius gibbosus*)

Sei whale or Rudolphi's rorqual
(*Balaenoptera borealis*)

Common rorqual or fin whale
(*Balaenoptera physalus*)

Blue whale
(*Balaenoptera musculus*)

Lesser rorqual
(*Balaenoptera acutorostrata*)

Humpback whale
(*Megaptera novaeangliae*)

Pygmy right whale
(*Neobalaena marginata*)

Greenland right whale
(*Balaena mysticetus*)

Biscay right whale
(*Eubalaena glacialis*)

WHALE HUNTERS OF THE NORTH-WEST
The Indians on the Pacific coast of America were excellent hunters of cetaceans. This is a reconstruction of an attack made from a canoe of the Makah tribe against a grey whale, *Eschrichtius gibbosus*.

Once there were large schools, but now just a few stray whales

In the ten-year period 1960–70 the whales killed, mostly by Japanese and Soviet ships, totalled over 600,000. International agreements to control the hunting seasons, also the species, numbers and minimum sizes of the cetaceans that could be caught were never respected. The Japanese maintain that their country has to take protein from the sea to feed their large population. But until recently other countries used whalemeat for the manufacture of dog and cat foods!

The first contacts between prehistoric man and whales probably took place when the creatures became stranded on the shore. Hunting started long afterwards and for obvious reasons the victims must have been cetaceans of the "floating" species, that is those which do not sink after they are killed: the Biscay right whale, the Greenland right whale and the sperm whale. In Europe the Basques of the 12th century were the first to hunt whales by striking them with fishing-spears. This profitable activity attracted the attention of the French, the English, the Dutch and, later on, the Russians and the Americans. In time large fleets were formed; in 1846 the number of Yankee whalers alone numbered 736.

Whaling ship of the United States from the middle of the last century. It carried six jolly-boats on board for the hunters.

SLOW RECOVERY

Regarded as extinct until just a few years ago, the Greenland right whale, *Balaena mysticetus*, for a long time the favourite catch of the whalers, had become very rare even in the last century because it was so mercilessly hunted. The species is now recovering slowly and there appear to be over a thousand of these whales in existence.

THE TOOLS OF THE TRADE

The crews of the whalers in the last century, especially the North American ones, were made up of men of all races and nationalities. Both the harpooner who threw the harpoons and the man in charge of the boat who killed the whale with a long spear were chosen from among the strongest and bravest seamen. This dangerous occupation has practically come to an end. The work is done more efficiently by a harpoon-gun mounted in the bows of the fast whalers.

Modern methods adapted to an ancient hunting pursuit

The gradual extermination of these gigantic mammals with the development of steam navigation shifted hunting activity from the northern to the southern hemisphere, into the seas of the Antarctic which were teeming with whales.

The adoption of the gun invented in 1865 by the Norwegian Svend Foyn, which could fire an explosive head, added to the carnage. As well as these innovations, factory-ships for processing the cetaceans at sea were built in the twenties. The fate of the whales was sealed by the introduction of such modern equipment as radar and sonar devices, and helicopters for reconnaissance; the poor cetaceans, obliged to surface in order to breathe, have no means of escape.

Spear about four metres long used to finish off the whale.

Harpoon of 1830, with an oak handle.

THE FLOATING FACTORY

An up-to-date factory-ship. Up top in the stern is the helicopter landing-deck; down below a whale, already slung up, is being taken in to be slaughtered. The harpooning of cetaceans is carried out from whaling vessels like the one in the foreground.

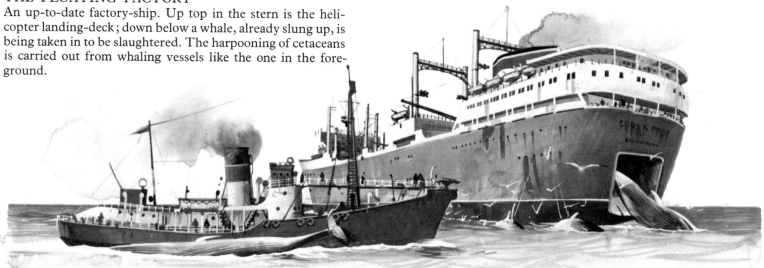

The red sea of the Faeroes

"Whales in sight!" When that announcement is made on the Danish Faeroe Islands to the north of the British Isles, houses, schools and offices are abandoned, shops are shut, and men arm themselves with harpoons and run to the boats, while the women and children crowd on to the shore to watch one of the most pointless massacres of animal life still going on at the present time. Having made their way out to sea, the islanders surround a school of black pilot whales, *Globicephala melaena*, whose instinct impels them to follow their leader.

After wounding some of them and so spreading panic among the group, the hunters pursue the pilot whales, forcing them to go aground on the shore, where they can easily be killed. The slaughter of the pilot whales, which constituted an essential part of the Faeroese economy in the past, is no longer justified in these more affluent times. But this gory festival of the sea, which accounts for three thousand victims every year, still goes on, because it forms a part of their deep-rooted local traditions.

TRUE SEALS
AND ELEPHANT SEALS—
HUNTED AT ALL LATITUDES

The most likeable and best known of the sea mammals, the seal, is even now, after being hunted for several thousand years, one of the animals most victimized because of its flesh, its blubber, the oil obtained from it and, in particular, its valuable fur. In the past the slaughter of these pinnipeds reached horrifying proportions (687,000 were killed in 1831!). In the last century the population of many species of seal fell to just a few hundred. Fortunately, the more advanced countries have passed laws controlling seal-hunting and the first signs of recovery are now becoming evident.

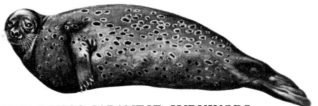

THE RUSSO-JAPANESE SURVIVORS
Distributed over the Soviet islands of the same name and to the north of the Japanese island of Hokkaido, the common Kurile seal, *Phoca vitulina kurilensis*, now protected, survives in scattered herds amounting to little more than 3000—all that are left after the concentrated hunting of the earlier days.

LITTLE IN DEMAND
The fur of the banded or ribbon seal, *Histriophoca fasciata*, is not highly prized by the North American market, and only the Eskimos catch it. In Asia, on the other hand, the Japanese kill it as a source of meat, oil and leather. Zoologists do not yet know much about this seal, solitary by nature, with a population ranging from 15,000 to 20,000. In winter it lives under the ice in which it makes holes, emerging from them to breathe.

THE LAST "MONKS"
The monk seals, *Monachus monachus*, of the Mediterranean, totalling just a few hundred, are seen from time to time on

the Balearic Islands, the Canaries, Madeira and the islands of the Aegean. In the Black Sea and on the north-west coasts of Africa they are more numerous, but they are clearly on the decline. A dozen were counted in Sardinia until just a few years ago; recent studies by The World Wildlife Fund have shown that only five or six are left.

THE WORLD HAS BEEN MOVED TO PITY

Every year, at the end of February, when the Harp seals, *Pagophilus groenlandicus*, have given birth to their young, called "white-coats" because of their very valuable white fur, the hunters appear and the massacre begins all over again. This was given wide publicity by the world press and television some time ago, and there was a chorus of indignant protests because of the cold-blooded brutality of the hunters, who skin the little creatures while they are still alive. This species is not in peril but, if the total number of "whities" killed every year is not halved, the position of the Greenland seal could become desperate.

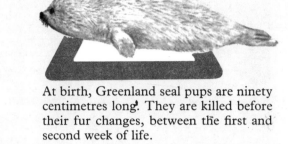

At birth, Greenland seal pups are ninety centimetres long. They are killed before their fur changes, between the first and second week of life.

A SMALL AND RARE DENIZEN OF THE ANTARCTIC

The smallest and rarest of the Antarctic seals, the Ross seal, *Ommatophoca rossi*, lives on the pack-ice, feeding on algae and molluscs. Over the entire South Pole area it is calculated that there are 20,000 still left. To prevent a further decline, the Antarctic Treaty nations have put these pinnipeds among the protected species, so that no more will be killed or captured.

THE PROTECTED ELEPHANTS

Although almost wiped out a hundred years ago, the elephant seals of the southern seas, *Mirounga leonina*, which are now protected, have started multiplying again. This species, the hunting and capture of which are restricted by law, numbers over half a million. Elephant seals are active mainly at night. They are massive, bulky creatures and adult males may actually reach 3600 kilograms in weight and 6·50 metres in length.

NORTHERN FUR SEALS

OFF EVERY YEAR TO THE PRIBILOF ISLANDS
When, towards the end of the 1700s, the Russian navigator Pribilof reached the islands which adopted his name, he discovered that this handful of rocks and promontories in the midst of the sea were used as rookeries by an astonishing number of northern fur seals, *Callorhinus ursinus*, nearly five million of them, representing the largest community of marine mammals in the whole of the northern hemisphere. The fur seals, in fact, migrate every year to the Pribilof Islands to give birth to their young. Slaughter by hunters had in less than half a century reduced the population of these pinnipeds, in 1914, to only 200,000. An international agreement was then drawn up and as a result of strict control the numbers of fur seals have been brought up to the present level of a million and a half, which is sufficient to guarantee the continuity of the species.

The number of northern fur seals allowed by a US Government commission to be killed every year ranges from 40,000 to 80,000. The killing is done by expert Aleutian hunters on the Pribilof Islands. The animals selected, young males aged three years, whose fur has not yet been marked by the scars of mating battles, are killed by clubbing on the skull. The young, the females and the old males are spared.

SOUTHERN FUR SEALS

1 Guadeloupe Fur Seal (*Arctocephalus philippi townsendi*)
2 Galapagos Fur Seal (*Arctocephalus australis galapagoensis*)
3 South African Fur Seal (*Arctocephalus pusillus*)
4 Juan Fernandez Fur Seal (*Arctocephalus philippi philippii*)

5 Kerguelen Fur Seal (*Arctocephalus tropicalis gazello*)
6 South American Fur Seal (*Arctocephalus qustralis*)
7 Australian Fur Seal (*Arctocephalus doriferus*)
(*Arctocephalus tasmanicus*)

ON THE VERGE OF EXTINCTION
Even the fur seals of Juan Fernandez, *Arctocephalus philippii*, with their valuable coats—there used to be millions of them on the archipelago of the same name off the coast of Chile—have been reduced almost to the point of extinction by indiscriminate hunting in the course of a couple of centuries. In just seven years three million fur seals were killed—a record figure in the history of the extermination of seals. The fur seal of Juan Fernandez is now protected by law and this should ensure the continuity of this breed.

MANY SPECIES IN TROUBLE
The various species of southern fur seal, except that of Guadeloupe, are distributed over the southern hemisphere. Nearly all these pinnipeds, with their very valuable furs, were the victims of prolonged and relentless persecution, and some species have now dwindled to only a few hundred. It is hoped that the steps taken by various governments to protect local species will enable large colonies to be rebuilt.

WALRUSES

When walruses were killed their ivory tusks were made into a variety of objects. Here you can see a hunting calendar.

AT THE MERCY OF THE ESKIMOS
The Atlantic walrus, *Odobenus rosmarus rosmarus*, is one of the marine mammals that is most seriously threatened. It has practically disappeared from the southern coasts of Greenland, the Svalbard Islands and the Arctic areas of Finland and is becoming rare in North America and Siberia. The remaining population, broken up into small groups dispersed over a vast distribution area, is at the mercy of the Eskimo hunters, the only people still allowed to kill these giants of the ice lands.

THE SEA OTTER— THE HISTORY OF A VALUABLE FUR

After hunting whales and seals, man came across another extraordinary aquatic mammal—a gentle and playful animal—the sea otter, *Enhydra lutris*, endowed by nature with a superb fur which has nearly led to its extinction.

In 1740 Russian explorers and adventurers began hunting these Mustelidae. The large figures paid for the fur of the sea otter also attracted the British, French, Portuguese and Americans. The wholesale carnage went on for a century and a half until, in 1911, the few remaining specimens were placed under protection. From that time onwards the species has been recovering slowly.

The sea otter lives permanently in the water, so its fur is thick at all seasons of the year. This gregarious animal, which is also an incomparable swimmer, only comes ashore when the sea is stormy, when it is threatened by grampuses and sharks or when the young are born. The babies are taken into the water at once and grow up there; they are suckled in the sea.

A SKELETON, A FEW DESCRIPTIONS AND NOTHING ELSE

Among the seals, Arctic foxes, sea otters and birds that inhabited an island in the North Pacific between Kamchatka and the Aleutian Islands, the sailors of a Russian ship wrecked on those coasts in 1741 were amazed to see a group of gigantic creatures eight or nine metres long wallowing about among the algae. These were sea mammals unknown to science, peaceful and harmless herbivores gregarious by nature and later referred to as Steller's sea-cows, *Hydroamalis stelleri*, after the name of their discoverer. In those days there would appear to have been two thousand of them; a mere twenty-seven years later the species was extinct as a result of the operations of Russian seamen and hunters in the Arctic. A few skeletons and the descriptions left to us by the German Steller are all that remains of this animal.

THE LAST OF THE SIRENS

When the sailors of Columbus caught sight of a female manatee, *Trichechus manatus manatus*, suckling her little one at the surface, they thought they had seen a siren. In those days manatees were plentiful in the seas and rivers of Central and South America, but centuries of hunting have radically reduced their numbers. Although they have been placed under protection, manatees have been harassed by poachers and their numbers are dwindling more and more.

THE SEA-COWS ON THEIR LAST REMAINING PASTURE

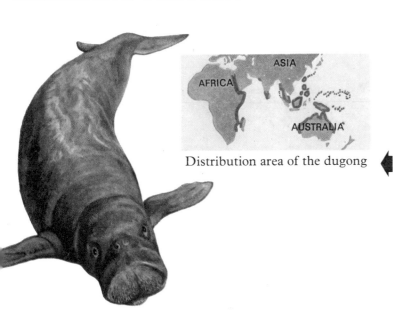

Distribution area of the dugong

IMPENDING EXTINCTION

An easy victim of hunters, who kill it with blows from a fishing-spear in the shallow waters close to the coast, the dugong, *Dugong dugon*, although protected in nearly all its distribution areas, is a species whose future is gravely threatened. Its flesh, rich in fat and oil, is highly valued, especially in the East, because of the curative and aphrodisiac properties attributed to it. Moreover, its skin is ideal for the manufacture of leather or glue. Finally, the numbers born do not make up for the dugongs killed, because their reproduction process is slow, so these massive, good-natured marine herbivores are definitely becoming extinct.

LIFE IN FRESH WATER

The position of certain species of marine fauna is in many cases alarming, but that of others living in inland waters or in their vicinity is even more critical. Whereas in the seas and oceans the decline in fauna is for the most part due directly to man and his marauding instincts, in fresh water he is indirectly responsible owing to the sad phenomenon of pollution belonging to our industrial era.

Indeed, if a certain level is exceeded, the dumping of industrial waste and of urban and agricultural refuse in watercourses has such a toxic effect that all forms of life in that important natural environment decline drastically in number.

DDT IS TO BLAME
The very handsome osprey, *Pandion haliaetus*, is a bird of prey found in Europe, North America, Asia and Africa. On the first two continents it is in danger of extinction owing to the sterility of its eggs. Traces of DDT, the terrible insecticide that has now been banned, have often been found in them.

NOW RARE
The Danube salmonoid called the huchen, *Hucho hucho*, which in recent times was common in the Danube, where specimens up to 1.5 metres long were caught, is now growing increasingly rare. This is due to pollution of the water and to the weirs built in the Danube and its main tributaries.

CHANGING SIDES
In Russia, too, water pollution has seriously damaged the country's fish resources. In the Caspian Sea the Russian sturgeon, *Acipenser guldenstaedti*, has migrated *en masse* towards the Iranian coast. This has had grave repercussions on the production of Russian caviare.

BLINDED BY POISON
The toxic garbage and effluent that have for some time been poured into the Adige, a river in northern Italy, which until only a few years ago was a flourishing fish reserve, have made the last of the graylings, *Thymallus thymallus*, living in its waters go blind. Their lack of sight is having a bad effect on the life of these fish, which need clean, oxygenated water.

FORCED TO MIGRATE

Synthetic detergents are widely found in domestic and industrial effluent, and in watercourses flowing into one another they not only poison the environment, but cause a decrease in the transparency of the water and an accumulation of foam at the surface. So many birds are unable to feed, the kingfisher, *Alcedo atthis*, for example, which is often forced to migrate in search of clearer water inhabited by fish.

SNARES AND TRAPS FOR THE OTTER

The soft, gleaming fur of the otter from the Cameroons, *Paraonyx microdon*, has attracted greedy hunters, who set snares and traps for this lovely aquatic mammal from Africa, so endangering the survival of the species.

ITS END IS NEAR

The Gila trout, *Salmo gilae*, a salmonoid fish belonging exclusively to the Gila river, which flows through New Mexico and Arizona, is becoming extinct owing to continual erosion and lowering of the waterlevel.

A SUBTERRANEAN LOSS

In deep wells and subterranean watercourses in the caves of Hays County, Texas, the Texan blind salamander, *Typhlomolge rathbuni*, which is very similar to the European proteus, is gradually disappearing, perhaps owing to pollution.

Among the species requiring immediate protection we can also include the La Plata dolphin, *Stenodelphis blainvillei*, a small dolphin reaching a maximum size of one metre and seventy centimetres. This aquatic mammal is common in the estuary of the River Plate and on the adjacent Atlantic coast and lives in turbid, muddy waters, but it goes on periodic migrations to the shores of Brazil, where it finds its way into the Lago dos Patos. The marked decline in the species is probably due to fishing and perhaps also to scarcity of the types of fish on which it feeds.

Rivers, lakes and marshes in the New World

THEIR FATE IS SEALED

The last grebes of the species *Centropelma micropterum* are attempting to evade complete extermination by hiding among the high cane-brakes on the shores and islets of icy Lake Titicaca in the Andes, at a height of 3800 metres. The fate of these unfortunate birds is sealed, for they are unable to fly and so can easily be disposed of.

IN THEIR LAST REFUGE

The draining of marshes, deforestation, the intensive use of agricultural pesticides and many years of hunting have inevitably reduced the numbers of swallow-tailed kites, *Elanoides forficatus*, which were spread over three-quarters of America fifty years ago. In 1973 the few survivors were concentrated in a restricted marshy area of Louisiana.

In the past, the traditional arrival of white storks, *Ciconia ciconia*, in European towns and villages was greeted as a good omen, a sign of well-being and prosperity. Their practice of nesting on roofs had given rise to the old legend of storks bringing babies.

Unfortunately, these large birds, which travel from Africa to Europe when they are about to breed, have for some time been an increasingly rare sight in our skies. There are many reasons for this, and they have not been fully explained scientifically.

But it is quite certain that changes in the natural environment in Europe and the danger of negotiating the many high-tension cables and chimney-stacks, also air traffic, atmospheric pollution, deafening noise and hunting, have forced the storks to change their accustomed route.

STORKS ON THE ROOF-TOPS:
a good omen since olden times

. . . if one day storks are seen flying over Europe again and their huge, basket-shaped nests appear once more in large numbers on the roofs of houses in Holland and Alsace and on the gables of homes in Baden-Württemberg and Styria, this will mean that man has indeed done something to renew the harmony of his age-old ties with nature.